THE *Ultimate* GUIDE TO TRUST DEED INVESTING

LEARN HOW TO EARN HIGHER RETURNS
& ACHIEVE STEADY CASH FLOW THROUGH
REAL ESTATE-BASED INVESTMENTS

Jordan Wirsz

CEO, Diamond Bay Investments

tandem
books

A Division of Palari Publishing

Library of Congress Cataloging-in-Publication Data

Wirsz, Jordan, 1983-
    The ultimate guide to trust deed investing : learn how to earn higher returns and achieve
steady cash flow through real estate-based investments / Jordan Wirsz.
        p. cm.
    ISBN-13: 978-1-928662-91-4 (pbk.)
    ISBN-10: 1-928662-91-9 (pbk.)
    1. Real estate investment--United States. 2. Mortgages--United States. 3. Investments--United
States. I. Title.

HD255.W57 2007
332.63'244--dc22

                                                          2007017627

Published by
Tandem Books
A division of Palari Publishing
1113 W. Main St.
Richmond, VA 23220

This publication is designed to provide accurate and authoritative information with regard to
the subject matter covered. It is sold with the understanding that the publisher is not engaged
in rendering legal, accounting, or other professional advice. If expert assistance is required, the
service of a competent professional should be sought.

Printed in the United States of America
10 9 8 7 6 5 4 3 2 1

Cover design: Ted Randler
Interior: Brian Bear
Editor: Donna Gregory

THE *Ultimate* GUIDE TO TRUST DEED INVESTING

LEARN HOW TO EARN HIGHER RETURNS & ACHIEVE STEADY CASH FLOW THROUGH REAL ESTATE-BASED INVESTMENTS

BY JORDAN WIRSZ

INVESTOR COMMENTS

"The return I'm making now…is a good, solid 12% return on my investment dollar."

"It's unfortunate I didn't stumble upon deed trust investing 25 years ago!"

"I make way more money now than I ever used to working for a living."

"It's hassle-free. I don't have to worry about a thing. I send the money and [they] send me my checks."

"I didn't have any surprises. I was very impressed."

"It's a great way to invest."

TABLE OF CONTENTS

CHAPTER 1

What is Trust Deed Investing?

If you've invested in the stock market in recent years, you've probably encountered your share of gains and losses. It's been a real-life roulette game as many stocks struggle to rebound in the midst of terrorism, war and volatile oil prices. Bonds and CDs—while offering security and steady returns—remain flat.

This unpredictable market has translated into a boom for some investors. Low interest rates have made real estate a sought-after commodity, prompting developers to take advantage of the strong economic demand. One can drive down countless streets and highways across America and see new shopping centers, office buildings, and other major construction projects where once there might have only been dirt and trees.

Wouldn't it be nice if you as an investor could somehow cash in on the success of these projects? Well, you can!

It's called trust deed investing, and it can yield double-digit returns while securing your investment through real estate.

OPPORTUNITIES EVERYWHERE

Every time you drive or walk through your neighborhood, chances are you've seen countless opportunities for financial gain without even realizing it. The next time you see steel going up for a new office building or notice a sign advertising reservations for the latest condominium complex, take a minute and think about how it's possible for those projects to come to fruition.

Where does the money come from to fund such a project? Do you think the developer really has enough money to bankroll such a venture himself? Not likely.

It's also unlikely that he would want to tie up all of his own money in such a project. Instead, he would want to keep his assets liquid so he could work on multiple projects simultaneously.

The chances are pretty good that the developer has a bank or private investors in the background feeding him funds to keep the project going. So, why would they do that? What's in it for the investors?

Higher returns! The developer pays his bank or his investors to use their money (in the form of a mortgage) and in most cases, they are paid very well.

Now, here's where you come in: You could be that investor.

WHAT IS A
TRUST DEED INVESTMENT?

Commercial and residential developers sometimes go to banks to fund their projects, but often they'll seek financing from a trust deed investment company.

(A word about terminology: Real estate loans are known as mortgages in the east and trust deeds in the west. For the purpose of this book, we'll focus on "trust deeds," but know that the two words are actually interchangeable.)

Where do trust deed investment companies get their money? From investors like you.

Trust deed investment companies are essentially middlemen between borrowers and investors. As middlemen, they search out the best deals for their investor pool and then use the money they raise to fund the projects with the greatest potential for making a solid return (with minimal risk)—often in the double digits. Yields can range widely, but typically fall between nine and twelve percent.

Now, you're probably saying, "That sounds great, but what's the catch? There's always a catch..."

As with nearly any investment option, investing in trust deeds is not guaranteed. In spite of how well a loan is underwritten, borrowers do sometimes default on their loans.

However, here is the beauty of trust deed investing: it offers a backup plan. Trust deed investing provides security for investors because it uses the real estate being lent on as collateral. If a loan defaults, the property can be foreclosed on, sold, and then the principal recovered is returned to the investors.

Trust deed investing is also less volatile than many other types of investments. For example, stock values vary depending on the day's news. Investors are at the mercy of the market if an oil pipeline bursts in Saudi Arabia or the Federal Reserve announces a hike in interest rates.

As an investment option, real estate is much more stable than stocks or other investments. When investing in trust deeds, borrowers may go bankrupt, but properties do not!

Trust deed investing has been around for as long as property has been bought and sold, and now you as an investor can add real estate to your portfolio without the complications of being a landlord or all of the administrative headaches that can make investing more of a burden than a pleasure.

HOW IT WORKS

When a borrower takes out a loan for a real estate project, he signs a promissory note and a deed of trust binding the property to the loan.

The promissory note is a contract between the trust deed investor and the developer where the developer promises to repay the loan. The deed of trust is a formal record of the transaction and is filed and recorded at the appropriate county recorder's office in the state in which the property is located.

Trust deeds can be placed in first, second, or even third lien positions. The first lien position is the most advantageous position since it takes priority over all others. Second and third lien positions are secondary to other liens that came before them, meaning they are riskier since they're honored after the first lien is repaid. However, since they place an investor or bank in a position of greater risk, they also tend to pay higher interest rates as compensation for assuming that risk.

It works similar to if you have a first and second mortgage on your home. Typically, you'll pay a higher interest rate on the second mortgage since the mortgage company is in a riskier lending position. If you stop making payments and the home is foreclosed on, the first mortgage usually receives any earnings from the sale before the company that holds the second mortgage because they're first in line to be paid.

A bit about second mortgages: having a second mortgage on a property you're investing in is not necessarily a bad thing. As an investor who is placing your money in a first trust deed, you're concerned about the borrower performing and making his payments to you. However, if the borrower takes out a second mortgage on that property, the company that holds that second mortgage MUST keep the first mortgage current in the event of a borrower default in order to maintain their position and right to receive proceeds from a sale. In other words, if the first isn't paid, the company holding the second MUST pay it or they will forfeit their right to recoup any funds. That's GREAT news for an investor on a first trust deed, because the second in such a case is providing added security!

WHO ARE THE BORROWERS?

Commercial and residential developers aren't the only ones who seek loans from trust deed investment companies, although they are the most common. Borrowers may also include builders, short-term property investors looking for funds for a time-sensitive purchase, investors needing short-term capital from their current properties, divorce buyouts, and those seeking funding for property rehabilitation projects.

The most common types of trust deed projects include income properties such as apartment buildings, office buildings and warehouses, land and vacant lots, and construction/development loans. First trust deeds are also commonly used to finance single-family homes, as well as multi-unit developments of town-homes and condominiums.

Trust deeds are also used to fund more unusual projects, such as theme parks, golf courses, health clubs, and churches. These aren't typical though, and as an investor, you should very carefully consider whether to invest your dollars into such projects.

Why?

Because while raw land, shopping centers, condos, and office buildings are bought and sold all the time, how many people are in the market to buy a knock-off of Walt Disney World or their own personal 18-hole golf course in rural Virginia? These types of projects offer less security for investors because there's less de-mand for them in the marketplace.

HIGHER RATE OF RETURNS

Anyone who has ever stood in line at the bank can probably guess why borrowers sometimes bypass tra-ditional funding institutions and instead choose to work with trust deed investment companies. Banks can be notoriously slow and bureaucratic, and those two qualities just don't work when a borrower wants to move on a deal.

Unlike the prompt decision you and I receive from a lender when we go to purchase a home, it can take up to 120 days—and sometimes even much longer—for a bank to fund a commercial real estate loan. In contrast, trust deed investment companies typically close a loan in much less than 30 days. Some loans have closed in as little as three days! This does not mean a trust deed company does not look at the same loan criteria as a bank…in fact, the underwriting process is very much the same. However, a trust deed investment company will do the same due diligence many times faster than any bank will.

Part of the reason trust deed investment companies are more fluid is because they aren't tied to lending rules and regulations like banks. There's no limit on how much money a trust deed company can loan out to one borrower or in one region, and lending terms are often more flexible.

Since trust deed companies are more fluid in responding to the market, borrowers often turn to them as a friendly alternative to traditional lenders, and they are prepared to pay a higher interest rate for this convenience.

It really comes down to supply and demand. If Dave the developer needs money to build a new luxury apartment building and he needs it fast, he'll often agree to pay a higher interest rate in order to move forward on his project. Dave can justify paying the higher rate since most trust deeds are for short-term financing. The norm is six months to two years, which is far shorter than the 30-year mortgage you're probably used to hearing about.

Short-term financing through a trust deed investment company buys the borrower some time to shop around with banks and other financial firms and negotiate a lower interest rate if he needs financing for a longer term. In the short term, however, the project gets funded quickly and the developer is able to keep his project moving.

If the borrower does secure long-term financing somewhere else, he pays back the loan to the trust deed investment company, which prompts the return of principal to the investors in that loan, and the pleasant surprise of an early payoff!

Many projects don't require long-term financing though. Developers typically like to finish a project quickly, sell it off, make their money, and then move on to another project—kind of like what trust deed investing allows you to do!

CHAPTER 2

A Solid
Investment

There are many investment choices today: stocks, bonds, mutual funds, CDs, precious metals, real estate, and others. Trust deed investing offers some advantages other investment options don't. In investment circles, security is important, but so are returns. Trust deed investing offers both.

COLLATERAL

When you invest in a trust deed, the loan is secured with tangible collateral: the property on which the loan is being written.

Why is that a good thing?

A collateralized loan means there's less chance of losing your investment dollars since the property can be sold to repay the loan.

There's the common practice of "cross-collateralization." Trust deed investment companies can secure your investment dollars even more in some cases by cross-collateralizing loans, or using more than one piece of property as collateral for the loan.

What that means is that if the borrower defaults on his loan, the investors not only retain ownership of the property that's being financed but can also claim an interest in the other properties that were used as collateral as well. While this practice isn't appropriate for every loan scenario, it is a term you should become familiar with as it will appear on investment offerings occasionally.

INTEREST RESERVE

Some trust deed companies also use a practice called "interest reserve" to further minimize risks. Through interest reserve, a certain number of the borrower's payments are automatically funded into the loan at closing, giving the borrower enough time to develop or sell the property without cutting into their cash flow by making large monthly payments. Since cash flow in the development industry is inherently unpredictable due to the ebb and flow of projects, the practice of interest reserve further safeguards the loan and gives both the borrower and the investor a leg up. While interest reserve isn't used in every loan, it does provide additional security to investors when appropriate.

HIGHER RETURNS

The overall real estate market has grown and appreciated in value over the years. Although occasional slow-downs do occur, the real estate market typically rebounds and recovers quickly in comparison to stocks or other investment opportunities. That makes real estate a strong contender when considering your investment options and strategy for achieving your personal financial goals.

Trust deed investing offers other merits as well. First, it provides monthly cash flow to investors. It works like your own home mortgage. Each month when you pay your mortgage, your payment is actually divvied up between principle, taxes and insurance, and interest. Trust deed investing follows a similar formula. As a trust deed investor, when a borrower sends in his payment each month, you'll receive a pro-rata share of that payment.

That income shows up with minimum effort. Unlike stocks, you aren't required to watch the markets each day and shift your holdings around according to how certain stocks are faring. With trust deed investments, you aren't required to play landlord (unlike when you personally own a property) and concern yourself with collecting the rent every month. Not only that, you don't have to cringe when you pick up the phone at 11 o'clock on a Friday night and your tenant says his second floor toilet has overflowed!

Instead, the trust deed investment company handles nearly every aspect of servicing the loan for you—from collecting and distributing payments to dissolving the loan when it's paid off. If for any reason the loan does go into default, they even handle the foreclosure and sale of the property in order to expedite the return of your funds.

RISK MANAGEMENT

Like nearly all investments, trust deed investing does involve some risk. From time to time, borrowers do default on their loans.

Due to the inherent risks, trust deed investments aren't the right solution for everyone. If you're a new investor with minimal liquid assets, you'll probably want to gain more experience and grow your portfolio and cash reserves before exploring trust deed investments.

Who is the ideal trust deed investor? If you are an individual or entity with adequate financial means that doesn't rely on their investment dollars for monthly income or need immediate access to their money, then you may want to consider trust deeds as a component of your investment strategy.

Most trust deed investment companies do require a minimum investment, which varies from firm to firm. This does many things, among which are making sure the investment is appropriate and help minimize administrative costs when it comes to servicing a loan. I'm sure you can imagine that it's more effective for a firm to have 25 investors with $100,000 each fund a $2.5M loan as opposed to 100 investors with $25,000 each!

For investors looking to grow their wealth in the early and middle stages of their investment years, trust deed investing helps diversify their portfolios while also providing steady growth. Investors who have shifted to preserving and generating income from their accumulated wealth can use the monthly income from their trust deed investments as a residual income stream.

MORE ABOUT RISKS

Trust deed investing is not insured by the FDIC or SIPC, so it does not offer any government protection like many bonds or CDs. Additionally, trust deed investment companies cannot guarantee any investment. Although most trust deed investment companies are diligent in researching risks through the underwriting process before approving loans to offer to their investors, it is up to the investor to make the final decision on whether to invest in a particular trust deed.

While real estate has historically provided solid returns, there are always general risks associated with any real estate-based investment, including uncertain fluctuations in general and local economic conditions, property values, interest rates, supply and demand, and governmental rules and regulations.

There are also risks associated exclusively with the borrower. A borrower's ability to repay a loan can change at any time. That's why it is important to work with a trust deed investment company that looks for potential risks during the underwriting process to minimize the chances that a borrower might default on a loan.

Conducting due diligence by carefully studying a borrower's credit history, financial statements, assets, employment history and other critical details help trust deed investment companies screen out borrowers who may not offer the best possible risk vs. reward scenario.

However, the primary consideration in any trust deed investment should be the collateral, as opposed to the credit of a borrower, because at the end of the day, the collateral is what will be sold to recoup investor funds. This concept may take some getting used to as an investor, as we live in a credit-based lending society. However, when you begin evaluating trust deed opportunities, start by looking at the property you'd be investing in and think: how easy would this be to sell if the borrower doesn't make his payments? That alone is the primary consideration, as trust deed investment firms aren't in the business of acquiring real estate. They are in the business of lending on real estate for a reasonable rate of return, and will do everything possible to make sure their investors keep coming back.

While diligent underwriting can help a trust deed investment firm identify potential risks associated with a particular loan, loans can default in spite of best-laid plans. Natural disasters, loss of cash flow, family emergencies, and other challenges can impact a borrower's ability to repay a loan—and affect your return on investment. There is no way to predict that a borrower will be injured when he's hit by a dump truck on the construction site or that a tsunami is going to hit the Gulf Coast and level the framework for a new hotel.

When unexpected challenges occur, monthly investor disbursements can be interrupted, and in extreme situations, the trust deed investment company may be forced to foreclose on the secured property. Although foreclosure is a fairly straightforward process in most cases, it does take time and money and that will frequently impact the bottom line on your returns in those instances.

If a property is foreclosed on, it is possible that it might not bring enough at auction to repay what's owed on the loan, resulting in a loss of principal for investors. As well, it may not sell at auction and the investors may own the property for what was owed on it. In such a case, there are various exit strategies that the trust deed firm can help negotiate to cure the situation. Although this is rare, it is important for investors to realize that it remains a possibility.

CHAPTER 3

A Good Fit

f you've been in investment circles for long, you've probably heard the mantra, "Diversify, diversify, diversify." This bears repeating when it comes to trust deed investing.

You wouldn't sink your entire retirement account into one stock trading on the New York Stock Exchange. The same holds true for trust deeds.

Investors should treat this form of investing as one more option—but not the only option. As exciting as trust deed investing can be, that doesn't mean you should go out and cash in all of your stocks and bonds and invest your entire net worth with a trust deed investment company.

Likewise, you should also avoid investing in only one trust deed or focusing on one geographic region for your investments. The reason for this is obvious: the more projects and regions you invest in, the more you reduce your risk. Statistically, investing in numerous profitable projects will usually offset one project that doesn't perform as expected.

After all, what's going to happen if you sink all of your investment dollars into building new high rises in a single city and a freak earthquake hits that metropolis, sending steel tumbling along with your investment dollars? Unforeseen events happen.

(Remember Hurricane Katrina?)

You should apply the "diversify" mantra within trust deed investing in the same way you would apply it to your stocks, bonds, and mutual funds. It's always a good idea to invest in several trust deeds so that if one borrower defaults on a loan, you may suffer a loss, but you haven't lost everything.

This is a good time to discuss the two general types of trust deeds: individualized and fractionalized.

INDIVIDUALIZED TRUST DEEDS

An individualized trust deed involves one investor investing in a single loan. Since the average investor usually doesn't have enough capital to bankroll an entire loan, this type of trust deed isn't the norm.

Individualized trust deeds offer several advantages. First, you know exactly where your money is going, and you retain ultimate control on how the loan is handled without having to weigh the interests of your fellow investors. Plus, individualized trust deeds make it easier for you to research and track the investments that suit your own needs.

They are also a single asset, so diversification is important. It's similar to investing in the stock market. You would want to buy stock in a wide range of companies, and ideally, purchase stock in several different sectors to further diversify your risk.

You'll want to follow a similar formula when investing in individualized trust deeds. By investing in various types of projects located in different regions, you minimize your risks.

FRACTIONALIZED TRUST DEEDS

Fractionalized trust deeds involve multiple investors funding one loan. These are more typical in the world of trust deeds.

Investors typically purchase units of a fractionalized trust deed and then share in the profits, expenses, and losses proportionately with their fellow investors.

TRUST DEED POOLS/FUNDS

A trust deed fund, or mortgage pool, is the latest option in trust deed investing. Essentially, a trust deed fund works like a mutual fund: there are multiple investors investing in multiple projects.

Mortgage pools clearly offer some advantages that individualized and fractionalized trust deeds do not. Many pools/funds are automatically diversified, meaning your risks are inherently minimized in those products. If one project defaults, the earnings from the other projects help offset any loss or decrease in yield.

Secondly, your investment is always at work in a pool since the trust deed company is always underwriting new loans as previous loans are paid-off. This is particularly good for beginning investors since any earnings can automatically be invested back into the pool, taking advantage of compounding.

As with all investments, there are also disadvantages to trust deed funds. Investors don't get to hand-select which projects they want to invest in, and due to compliance costs, returns are usually slightly less than individualized or fractionalized trust deeds.

WHAT TO LOOK FOR

Many companies are now moving in the direction of offering trust deed funds/pools now since they allow a larger demographic of investor to participate. Trust deed funds are also easier on investors because they are less paperwork-intense investments than fractionalized deeds of trust.

They aren't perfect though. A pool is only as good as the trust deed company that's managing it. In the past, some trust deed funds/pools have gone under due to fraud among their managers. That shouldn't deter investors, though. It just means investors should do their research before selecting a fund and/or trust deed firm.

When researching trust deed companies, look for those that offer federally registered funds. Generally, companies that deal in federally registered funds are more substantial and stable. Read each company's prospectus very carefully and ask questions when you don't understand something that's being presented or explained to you.

CHAPTER 4

How to
Choose
a Trust Deed

How do you know if a particular loan is a good investment? The primary goal of any trust deed investment company should be to originate and fund loans that involve minimal amounts of risk while generating favorable rates of return. Trust deed investment companies do this by evaluating several factors, the most important of which is loan-to-value (LTV) ratio.

DETERMINING LTV RATIO

You may have heard of LTV before if you've ever secured a mortgage for buying a home. In the case of a home mortgage, LTV fluctuates depending on the amount of the down payment and the property's market value. The larger the difference between a home's market value and the amount a borrower owes on the property, the more likely a mortgage company is to fund the loan.

For example, let's say you want to buy a home for $200,000 and you plan to use $20,000 as a down payment. In that scenario, your LTV would be 90 percent.

Since most mortgage companies prefer a LTV of 80 percent or lower, your lender might charge you a higher interest rate and require you to carry mortgage insurance as a way of decreasing their risks. If you default on the loan, the mortgage company wants to be able to sell the property for enough money to pay off what you owe on the loan (and maybe even make a profit).

The same holds true for trust deed investing. Most trust deed investment companies like to see a LTV of 70 percent or less depending on the particular project. The 70 percent threshold is advantageous for investors since it reduces risk by providing at least a 30 percent cushion of equity, which can then be used to recover costs associated with default on the loan.

To further explain, say a property is valued at $100,000 and the borrower wants to take out a loan for $70,000. That means the property already has $30,000 in equity, or a 70 percent LTV.

From a financial standpoint, that's a pretty good deal. If the loan is paid off on-time, the investors have made a comfortable rate of return on the interest paid by the borrower. If the borrower defaults on the loan, the chances are great that the investors will be able to resell the property for more than 70 percent of the property's market value. So, if the property sells at auction for more than $70,000, the investors will typically still make a profit even though the borrower has defaulted. This is a win-win scenario for investors, regardless of whether the borrower repays the loan or not.

OTHER WAYS TO REDUCE RISK

To further reduce risk, many trust deed investment companies require a personal guarantee, meaning the borrower is personally responsible for any capital loss due to foreclosure. Then there are other safeguards such as hazard insurance and impound accounts. Any land containing a structure is usually required to carry hazard insurance naming the investors as beneficiaries in case of fire or other potential structural damage.

Impound accounts are set up for some loans. These accounts automatically set aside a portion of each monthly payment for property taxes, insurance premiums and other fees and work similar to an escrow account on a home mortgage.

EVALUATING PROJECTS

When evaluating potential trust deed investments, there are several key points to consider.

First, look at the property. The general philosophy of trust deed companies is "loan to own," meaning they tend to only fund loans on properties that will be easy to resell in the event that they have to take the property back through foreclosure.

Your trust deed investment company should always obtain an independent appraisal that determines the property in question's replacement cost, market or sales value, and/or income value. Additionally, if a property is income-producing (i.e. it's an apartment building or other property that is leased to tenants), the appraisal should include a survey to determine present and potential rental income.

Again, LTV is extremely important. A reputable trust deed investment company will only fund projects with a comfortable LTV margin that ensures the likelihood of full recovery if the borrower defaults on the loan. LTV is generally expressed in a percentage—the lower the LTV, the better.

OTHER CONSIDERATIONS

LTV isn't the only criteria to consider. Trust deed investment companies screen the borrower's credit report, financial and income statements, assets, obligations, and the prospective plans for the property. It's also important to consider the borrower's ability to repay the loan. They also look closely at the type of property involved, the feasibility that the project will be successful, potential complications should the loan go into foreclosure, and other factors that might impact potential value.

WHAT TO ASK FOR

Most trust deed investment companies provide potential investors with a standardized packet of information for each loan for consideration. The most common documents include a loan summary and appraisal.

Make sure to study these documents closely. As an investor, you're the trust deed company's extra set of eyes. Ask questions. Don't just assume because the trust deed investment company is considering funding a project that you should consider it, too.

Every loan is not right for every investor.

COLLATERAL

How a loan is secured can also minimize risks. Look for projects that have cross-collateralization. These types of trust deeds are secured with multiple properties, potentially reducing risk for investors. Using multiple properties as collateral can create a better equity position (i.e. a lower LTV), and usually demonstrates a sincere intent on behalf of the borrower to repay the loan. If the borrower does default on the loan, the investors can then claim an interest in all of the collateralized properties, reducing the possibility of lost investment capital. Cross-collateralization is not always necessary or always available on every loan, but it is a tool a trust deed company can use to help provide additional security to investors.

LIEN POSITION

Lien position can be just as important as LTV and collateral. By having a first lien position, the validity of the loan is strengthened since it will be paid-off first in cases of default. A second or third lien position is less secure since that means investors are second or third in line to be paid back if the borrower fails to repay the loan.

As another safeguard, most trust deed investment companies require title insurance, which insures the lien position against any past or future liens placed against the property.

A FEW WORDS ABOUT SECOND TRUST DEEDS

Second (and third, etc.) trust deeds may pay greater returns, but they pose far more risk for investors.

There are special considerations when evaluating second trust deeds. It's critical for investors to look carefully at all available senior lien information. How much is owed on the first trust deed? What are the terms of the primary lien? Is the borrower facing pre-payment penalties or negative amortization? How old is the loan? Is the borrower current on all payments?

Use a common sense approach when considering these types of trust deeds. You'd probably think twice about loaning your brother $50,000 if you knew he was already two months behind in paying his mortgage payment. In that situation, you definitely wouldn't want to loan him the money unless you could afford to lose it.

The same is true for second trust deeds—only in the above example you can use family guilt as lever-age to get your money back from your brother should he default on the loan. In the world of trust deed in-vesting, you won't have that kind of leverage. You'll have to wait until the investors who hold the first trust deed have their payday before you get yours—that is, if there's anything left after they are paid off.

ANOTHER WORD OF CAUTION

Trust deeds beneath the second position are extremely risky, as are trust deeds without title insurance and properties with environmental issues. Be wary of these types of investments and use common sense when evaluating them.

EXIT STRATEGY

Assessing how to get out of a trust deed is just as important as assessing why to get involved in the first place. Don't invest in a trust deed without knowing the exit strategy. How does the borrower intend to repay his trust deed loan? He may be in the processes of securing permanent, long-term financing through a traditional lender or may intend on selling the property. The exit strategy should be clearly stated on the offering, and if it is not, ask the trust deed firm how the borrower intends to settle his loan at the end of the term.

CHAPTER 5

Taking Care
of Business

Once a trust deed investment company closes a loan, it will be monitored by a loan servicing company or their internal servicing department from inception to payoff. Loan servicing involves collecting monthly payments, ensuring all taxes and insurance premiums are paid regularly, mailing balloon payment notices to borrowers as required by law, communicating with the borrower, handling the loan payoff, and making sure all documentation is kept in order.

If a borrower defaults on his loan, the loan servicing company or servicing department is responsible for attempting to collect the debt and following through on foreclosure if necessary. If the property is foreclosed on and does not sell at auction, the trust deed company should then locate a realtor to sell the property, and coordinate any repairs or improvements that might increase marketability.

Depending on which trust deed investment firm you're working with, loan servicing may be handled in-house or by a third-party servicing firm.

ADVANTAGES OF IN-HOUSE

In-house servicing offers some clear advantages for investors. Most importantly, the same trust deed investment company that looks out for its investors on the front-end is also more likely to have its investors' interests at heart during the loan servicing process. Because an outside firm is not an actual stakeholder in the transaction, they often are not in tune with investors' needs.

In some ways, it's equivalent to banking with a national chain versus having your personal accounts handled by a neighborhood credit union. Generally, the neighborhood credit union is going to be more diligent about addressing your concerns as a customer since it's a two-way relationship: you depend on the credit union to safeguard your checking and savings accounts and the credit union depends on you for its survival in the marketplace.

Familiarity is another advantage of in-house servicing. If servicing is handled in-house, then the trust deed investment company is intimately familiar with the details of the loan as well as the investors who have chosen to participate, and thus more likely to keep investors in the loop should difficulties arise.

CHAPTER 6

The Business
of Loan Defaults

L ike most investments, there is no guarantee that a borrower is going to pay back a loan. If the borrower fails to repay the loan as promised, the deed of trust allows the investors to file a "notice of default" and start the foreclosure process. If the borrower fails to repay the loan by the time the property goes to foreclosure, then the property is auctioned at a foreclosure sale. Proceeds from that sale are used to repay the loan. If for any reason the property doesn't sell at auction, then the investors own that property. In that case, the trust deed investment company will typically assist investors in selling the property.

THE FORECLOSURE PROCESS

While foreclosure may be a scenario that sounds pretty harrowing, the actual process is fairly straightforward. It involves a little coordination between the trust deed investment company representing the investor(s), the title company, an attorney, and any other third parties providing services.

When a borrower first misses a payment, the entity providing the loan servicing will attempt to reach the borrower via phone or through the mail in order to collect the delinquent payment. If the borrower fails to bring the loan back into good standing then a "non-judicial foreclosure process" is initiated. (A non-judicial foreclosure process does not involve the court system, while a judicial foreclosure does.) Some states require judicial foreclosures.

First, a "notice of default" is filed between 10 and 45 days after the due date of the loan payment. The notice is then recorded at the appropriate county recorder's office, and the title company or attorney proceeds with foreclosure.

If the notice of default is filed because the loan term has matured without payment, the investors may require the full principle amount to be paid in full at any time throughout the foreclosure process. However, if the foreclosure proceedings are due to the borrower not making his monthly payments, then the investors have the option of either reinstating the loan or requiring the borrower to pay it in full.

A one- to three-month reinstatement period is sometimes required before a "notice of sale" can be published and recorded. The notice indicates the time, date and place of the sale. Foreclosure procedures and laws vary on a state by state basis. The property can then be sold at public auction to the highest bidder. Up to five days prior to the auction sale, the trust deed company will continue to try to collect on the debt.

Just prior to the sale, the property should be inspected and appraised to determine its condition and value. These factors can be used to help determine a starting bid price.

During the sale, there are three ways to open bidding on a property. A full credit bid is the most common way since it covers the full total amount owed to investors including principle, accrued interest, late fees, legal fees, foreclosure fees and other expenses.

An under-bid is when the opening bid is less than the total amount due on the loan. In some cases, the starting bid is the amount of outstanding principle on the loan. Any amount over that is credited to the investors to cover costs.

The costs associated with foreclosures vary depending on the loan and the state in which the property is located. If no one bids on the property, the title is conveyed to the investors for the opening bid and the trust deed company then helps the investors resell the property at a later date.

CHAPTER 7

Some
Final Words

The information included here should provide you with a solid knowledge base as you consider whether trust deeds are right for your investment portfolio. While there are a great many things to consider as you begin to evaluate trust deed opportunities and the firms that offer them, the process is fairly simple. A single investment provides monthly interest payments for a pre-determined length of time, and you can add the benefits of real estate-based investments to your portfolio without the complications of being a landlord.

Take your time, ask questions, and become familiar with the firm where you're considering placing your investment dollars. As important as the returns is the level of customer service you receive as an investor. Do you have a single point of contact? Do they return your phone calls and emails promptly? Are they willing and available to help educate you as you become familiar with their firm's procedures and the process involved in trust deed investments?

Trust deed investing, in addition to providing superior rates of return for short-term investments, is a great diversification tool for your investment portfolio that has thousands of satisfied investors already. Isn't it time for you to take the first step?

About
the Author

J ordan Wirsz is the Chairman and CEO of Diamond Bay Investments Inc., a firm specializing in private real estate lending and investments.

Jordan made his first trust deed investment with profits he earned after selling an aviation business in Florida. As he watched his investment dollars grow, he became less of a skeptic and more of a believer in trust deed investing and how it can offer steady, solid returns with minimal risk.

As his knowledge about the private lending industry and real estate grew, he expanded his own real estate portfolio by buying various types of properties. After buying and selling millions in real estate and continuing to invest in trust deeds, Jordan established Diamond Bay Investments in order to increase the size of loans he was able to underwrite by sharing the benefits of trust deed investing with other private investors.

Diamond Bay is a private money real estate lender that focuses primarily on funding loans on commercial real estate of varying types. As Diamond Bay's founder, Jordan now enthusiastically shares his own knowledge of this little-known type of investment that produces high yields and monthly cash flow with minimal risk. He is a published author and philanthropist, and is frequently sought after as a public speaker due to his recognition as a credible source for information on the real estate and private lending markets, as well as wealth-building strategies.

To this day, Jordan Wirsz remains a trust deed investor.

Jordan Wirsz
Chief Executive Officer
Diamond Bay Investments Inc.

Visit
www.DiamondBayInvestments.com
or
www.JordanWirsz.com

BUY DIRECT FROM PALARI

Save with free shipping on

The Maverick Millionaire

Jordan Wirsz

(ISBN-10: 1928662080)

$23.95, 6 x 9" hardcover

Jordan Wirsz started his first business with he was 14. Now, at the age of 24, he runs his own company, Diamond Bay Investments. He is also a speaker and philanthropist who inspires others to harness their own entrepreneurial spirit.

Remember FREE SHIPPING when ordered with this form!

Deliver books to:

Name_____

Phone_____-_____Email_____

Address_____

City_____State_____Zip_____

Number of Books　　　　Total

The Maverick Millionaire $23.95 @ _____ = _____

VA residents add 5.0% sales tax = _____

TOTAL ENCLOSED = _____

Order online at WWW.PALARIBOOKS.com
or send check or money order to
Palari Publishing
P. O. Box 9288
Richmond, Virginia 23227-0288